JESUS'
CHRISTMAS
PARTY

Nicholas Allan

HUTCHINSON

London   Sydney   Auckland   Johannesburg

For Richard McBrien

First published in 1991 by Hutchinson Children's Books
an imprint of the Random Century Group Ltd
20 Vauxhall Bridge Road, London, SW1V 2SA

Random Century Australia (Pty) Ltd
20 Alfred Street, Milsons Point, Sydney, NSW 2061, Australia

Random Century New Zealand Ltd
PO Box 40-086, Glenfield, Auckland 10, New Zealand

Random Century South Africa (Pty) Ltd
PO Box 337, Bergvlei, 2012 South Africa

Designed by Paul Welti
Printed in Hong Kong

British Library Cataloguing in Publication Data is available
ISBN 0-09-176 380-0

There was nothing
the innkeeper liked
more than a good
night's sleep.

But that night there was
a knock at the door.

'No room,' said the innkeeper.
'But we're tired and have travelled
through night and day.'
'There's only the stable round the back.
Here's two blankets. Sign the register.'
So they signed it: 'Mary and Joseph.'

Then he shut the door,
climbed the stairs,
got into bed,
and went to sleep.

But then, later, there was
another knock at the door.

'Excuse me. I wonder if
you could lend us
another, smaller blanket?'

'There. One smaller blanket,'
said the innkeeper.

Then he shut the door,
climbed the stairs,
got into bed,
and went to sleep.

But then a bright light
woke him up.

'That's *all* I need,'
said the innkeeper.

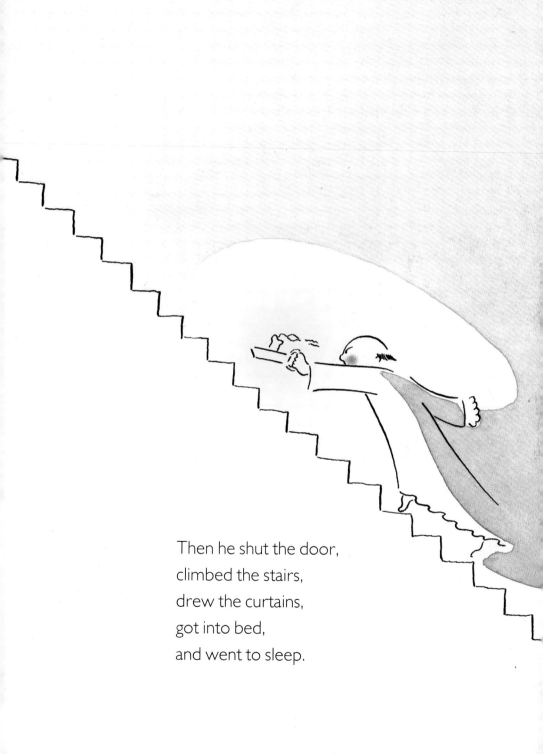

Then he shut the door,
climbed the stairs,
drew the curtains,
got into bed,
and went to sleep.

But then there was *another*
knock at the door.

'We are three shepherds.'
'Well, what's the matter? Lost your sheep?'
'We've come to see Mary and Joseph.'
'ROUND THE BACK,'
said the innkeeper.

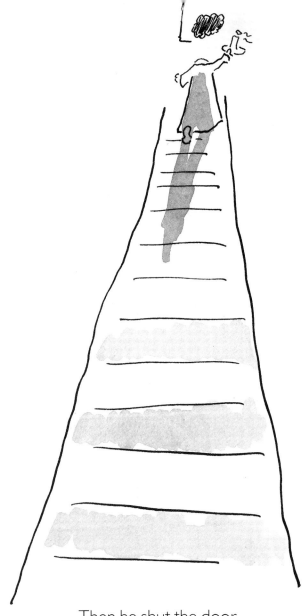

Then he shut the door,
climbed the stairs,
got into bed,
and went to sleep.

But then there was yet
another knock at the door.

'We are three kings. We've come —'

'ROUND THE BACK!'

He slammed the door,
climbed the stairs,
got into bed,
and went to sleep.

But **then** a chorus of
singing woke him up.

'RIGHT – THAT DOES IT!'

So he got out of bed,

stomped down the stairs,

threw open the door,

went round the back,

stormed into the stable, and was just about to speak when —

'Ssshh!' whispered everybody,

'**Baby?**' said the innkeeper.

'Yes, a baby has this night been born.'

'Oh?' said the innkeeper, looking crossly into the manger.

And just at that moment, suddenly, amazingly, his anger seemed to fly away. 'Oh,' said the innkeeper, 'isn't he *lovely!'*

In fact, he thought he was so special

so that they could come a

he woke up *all* the guests at the inn,

ʋe a look at the baby too.

So no one got much sleep that night!

THE END